THE LAMPLIGHTER

Jackie Kay was born in Edinburgh in 1961 to a Scottish mother and a Nigerian father, and adopted by a Scottish couple at birth. She grew up in Glasgow, and studied at Stirling University, where she read English.

She has published four previous collections with Bloodaxe, as well as *Darling: New & Selected Poems* (2007). *The Adoption Papers* (1991) won a Scottish Arts Council Book Award and a Saltire First Book of the Year Award; 'Black Bottom' (chapter 7 of the title-sequence) won the Forward Prize for best single poem; and the book was shortlisted for the *Mail on Sunday* / John Llewellyn Rhys Prize. She won a Somerset Maugham Award for her second collection, *Other Lovers* (1993). Her third collection, *Off Colour* (1998), a Poetry Book Society Special Commendation, was shortlisted for the T.S. Eliot Prize. Her fourth collection, *Life Mask* (2005), was a Poetry Book Society Recommendation, as is *Darling: New & Selected Poems* (Bloodaxe Books, 2007).

Her recordings include the cassette *The Poetry Quartets: 1* [with Simon Armitage, Kathleen Jamie & Glyn Maxwell] (British Council/Bloodaxe Books, 1998) and the CD *Jackie Kay reading from her poems* (The Poetry Archive, 2006). *The Lamplighter* was published by Bloodaxe in 2008 with a CD of the BBC radio play version of her acclaimed play/epic poem on slavery.

Her first novel, *Trumpet* (Picador, 1998), won the Guardian Fiction Prize, a Scottish Arts Council Book Award and the Author's Club first novel award. She has published two books of stories with Picador, *Why Don't You Stop Talking?* (2002) and *Wish I Was Here* (2006), which won her the Decibel Writer of the Year Award in 2007. She shared the volume *Penguin Modern Poets 8* (second series, 1996) with Merle Collins and Grace Nichols.

Her books for children include a novel, *Strawgirl* (2002), and four poetry collections: *Two's Company* (1992), *Three Has Gone* (1994), *The Frog Who Dreamed She Was an Opera Singer* (1998) and *Red, Cherry Red* (2007). She has won the Signal Poetry Award twice, in 1993 and 1999; and won the CLPE Poetry Award in 2008 for *Red, Cherry Red*.

Jackie Kay was given a Cholmondeley Award by the Society of Authors in 2003, and was made an MBE in 2006. A Fellow of the Royal Society of Literature, she is Professor of Creative Writing at Newcastle University. She has written widely for stage, radio and television, and lives in Manchester with her son.

JACKIE KAY

THE LAMPLIGHTER

BLOODAXE BOOKS

Text copyright © Jackie Kay 2007, 2008.
Audio recording copyright © BBC 2007:
A BBC Radio Programme licensed by the BBC.

ISBN: 978 1 85224 804 8

First published 2008 by
Bloodaxe Books Ltd,
Highgreen,
Tarset,
Northumberland NE48 1RP.

www.bloodaxebooks.com
For further information about Bloodaxe titles
please visit our website or write to
the above address for a catalogue.

Bloodaxe Books Ltd acknowledges
the financial assistance of
Arts Council England, North East.

LEGAL NOTICE

Cover design: Neil Astley & Pamela Robertson-Pearce.

Cover printing: J. Thomson Colour Printers Ltd, Glasgow.

Printed in Great Britain by
Bell & Bain Limited, Glasgow, Scotland.

THE LAMPLIGHTER

Jackie Kay's *The Lamplighter* was first broadcast by the BBC on Radio Three on Sunday 25 March 2007 with the following cast:

THE LAMPLIGHTER	Clare Perkins
BLACK HARRIOT	Aicha Kossoko
CONSTANCE	Martina Laird
MARY	Mona Hammond
MACBEAN	John Dougall
ANIWAA	Jordan Loughran
SINGER	Gweneth-Ann Jeffers
DIRECTOR	Pam Fraser-Solomon
ORIGINAL MUSIC	Dominique Le Gendre

For Pam Fraser Solomon
with love

Time with its murderous gums and pale, windowless throat,
Its mouth pressed to our mouths,
               Pushing the breath in, pulling it out.'

CHARLES WRIGHT: 'Time Will Tell.'

There are things one does not say for a long time, but once they are said, one never stops repeating them.

BENJAMIN CONSTANT: 'Adolphe', 1815

Scene 1: Interior Fort

The noise of the sea slapping against the walls of Cape Coast Castle.
The sound of many different African languages, talking fast, scared.

ANNIWAA:

I am a girl. I am in the dark. I don't know how long I've been
kept in the dark. High above me, there is a tiny crack of light.
Last time I counted, I was eleven, nearly twelve. I am a girl.
Last time I saw my mama, I was carrying a water gourd on my
head. The water was sloshing-sloshing all over my clothes. Mama
was clapping her hands and laughing at me. I am frightened of
the dark. I don't know where I am. I don't even know why I'm
here.

Once upon a time, I lived in a house with a cone-shaped roof,
in a big compound. My mother grew okra and pumpkin in her
yard. My father shaped woods and metals.

A time now ago, I had my hair just done fresh. Pretty, my Mama
say. Small sections coiled with thread. My brother and I were
playing and laughing. My brother says my laugh is funny and
that my laugh makes him laugh.

All of a sudden, some men come and take us. I know those
people. They have the marks on the face of the enemy. I kick
and scream and shout. Furious. They bundle us off through
the woods. Pushing and shouting. Move. Move. Beating us. I
hold on to my brother. My brother holds on to me.

We are dragged through the forest for days and nights and days.
It is a long time. I am tired and heavy as an elephant. I cry loud
for my Mama to hear me. I cry loud for my Papa to see me.

One day, we arrive here. A place that is bigger than the palace
of the Paramount Chief. Some call it a palace, a fort, a factory,
a prison, a dungeon. My brother is pulled away. I reach out
but I cannot hold him. My tears dry up inside me. My mouth

9

goes dry and my lips. My tongue sticks to the roof of my mouth. After that, I stop talking. The words dry under my lips.

Outside this place, where I am trapped and kept like an animal, there is a sound I never hear before. A crashing and thudding. They say it is The Sea. I think it is a wild monster. I think it is coming for me.

Scene 2: Shipping News

The voice of the Shipping Forecast will be interrupted by the voices of the four black women. These women form a chorus throughout the play. Behind their voices there's the roaring, crashing of the big Atlantic.

MACBEAN:

> There are warnings of gales
> In the Viking North.
> The general synopsis at midday – low.
> 971 moving steadily Northeast and filling.
> New High expected Trafalgar
> By the same time.

LAMPLIGHTER:

> By the same time.

MACBEAN:

> Saturday, August 11, 1707
> The weather in Liverpool was close.
> Gales running between the south and west.
> Dirty weather, the ship's captain said.
> The wild Aurora Borealis
> Flew around with unusual swiftness.
>
> The *Dorothy* reached Barbados, June 1709.
> One hundred slaves surviving.
> Veering North West 6 to 8.
> Occasionally severe Gale 9.
> The *Duke of Argyll* reached London
> Eighty slaves surviving. Soon.
> The moon that night was in a shroud.

CONSTANCE:

> The moon was in a shroud.

MACBEAN:

    The *Annapolis* reached London –
    Less than a third of the slaves survived.
    Captain's Log: 23rd May 1709 –
    Buryed a man slave No 84.
    Wednesday 29 May –
    Buryed a Boy slave, No 86 of a flux.
    Decreasing. Rough or very rough.
    The weather still dirty, the captain said.
    Slow moving, with little change.

BLACK HARRIOT:

    The weather filthy!

MACBEAN:

    Rain then showers. Moderate or rough.
    Thursday, 13 June 1709
    Buryed a woman slave, no 47.
    Later Decreasing.

BLACK HARRIOT:

    Into the howling, moaning Atlantic.
    Into the open-grave-green sea.
    Into the choppy waters, another body.
    Another stiff black wave into
    the tight black waves of the sea.
    Into the turbulent waters,
    another body yet.

MARY:

    If you want to learn to pray,
    Go to sea.

Scene 3: Interior Fort

ANNIWAA:

It smells bad down here. So bad I don't want to breathe. So bad, I take small sips of the dirty air.

Sometimes strange people come down. Their skin is pink. They look through me like they can't see me. The women are moaning but they can't hear us. The sounds they make with their mouth are strange. I don't know what they mean.

At first when they shove and push me down here, I am hungry, so hungry I am hollow. Now, I don't want to eat. I don't want to eat if I can't eat with my mama. A woman here, with the markings of the enemy, tries to feed me a little. At night I sleep under her arm like a bird under a wing. We are all crush-crush in here.

I am getting smaller by the day. I am a girl getting smaller. Maybe soon I will be the size of a goat and then the size of a yam and then the size of a cricket and then I will vanish. Maybe I will start to grow backwards. Soon I might be ten, then nine.

My hands are small and my legs are sticks.
My belly is swollen in a strange way. I can feel but I can't see myself. I can feel I am not myself.
When I get really scared, I try and make my Mama come for me.

I close my eyes and say it to myself. Please. Please. Come and find me. Come and get me. Please. I see her in my head. She is in the yard, pounding fufu. She is wrapping kankei cake in banana leaf. She is digging for yam. I can see her in her yellow head-tie. I see her walking through the trees, past the ones with the big curly leaves, past the wide one that is older than my grandmother. Striding like a giant. Coming to find me.

Then, all of a sudden, my mother is gone. I can hear the big monster howling at the thick dungeon walls.
Sometimes I can hear singing, strange singing.

13

Song: All

CONSTANCE, BLACK HARRIOT, MARY *and* THE LAMPLIGHTER *sing as if they are in the fort's chapel.*

ALL:

All glory be to God on high
And on earth be peace;
Good-will henceforth from heaven to men
Begin and never cease.

ANNIWAA:

One day slips into another day. The dark comes and folds up the days. I wonder if I will ever get out of here. I wonder if I will ever go home. I wonder if I will be a girl when I get out of here. A girl, twelve. Maybe a girl, thirteen. Fourteen. Maybe not a girl anymore. Maybe a woman. Maybe I'll have grown into a small woman without my mother.

Scene 4: Herself Talking

Exterior a place of memories. Caribbean countryside, Devon quayside and urban landscape. Cane field. Suggested rather than stated.

The same chorus of three women will accompany the telling of the Lamplighter's story, to give the impression that any single story is a multiple one.

FX:

> *(The sound of wind with the sound of sea on cobbles in the background added.)*

THE LAMPLIGHTER:

> Reader, be assured this narrative is no fiction.
> I have not written my experiences in order to attract attention to myself. On the contrary, my description falls far short of the facts. It is not my intention to horrify.

BLACK HARRIOT:

> This story was written by Herself.

MARY:

> This is Herself talking.

CONSTANCE:

> I am. She is. You are. They. They is. They are, they are, they are.

LAMPLIGHTER:

> Nobody ever told my story before.
> I was the one who was recaptured and sold
> For eighty pounds, on December 8th 1792,
> forced then to board a vessel at Lamplighter's Hall,
> Avonmouth, heading for the plantations.

BLACK HARRIOT:

> To board a ship and cross the water
> Board a ship and be carried over

To be carried across the water
And land with strangers all over,
All over again

MACBEAN:

I saw her –
Tears flowed down her face
Like a shower of rain.
The Inn where she was sold
Still stands on Station road,
Shirehampton, Avonmouth.
I saw her open mouth.
I saw the lost look in her teary eyes.

CONSTANCE:

Avonmouth, open mouth.

MARY:

We were sold in English Inns.

BLACK HARRIOT:

We were sold in Bristol coffee houses.
We were sold in Liverpool warehouses, shops, on the front steps
of Custom House, on the east side of the old dock.
At the slave ports of Lancaster, Whitehaven, PortsMOUTH,
PlyMOUTH, DartMOUTH

CONSTANCE:

Mouth, lips, teeth.

BLACK HARRIOT:

Exeter, Glasgow, CHESTer

CONSTANCE:

Chest, heart, lungs

MACBEAN:

To be sold by Auction at George's Coffee House, betwixt the hours of six and eight o'clock, a very fine Negro girl about eight years of age. Any person willing to purchase her may apply to Capt Robert Syers, Merchant Draper near the Exchange, where she may be seen till the time of sale.

BLACK HARRIOT:

We were sold for sugar in the coffee.
Sugar in the tea.

MARY:

We were sold for tobacco and rice.
Sold to make the cities rise.

MACBEAN:

To be sold for want of employment...a healthy Negor wench, of about 21 years old, she has a female child of nigh three years old, which will be sold with the wench, if required.

CONSTANCE:

Bristol, London, Birmingham, Liverpool, Manchester, Glasgow, Edinburgh

MACBEAN:

Horses, to be sold at the Bull and Gate Inn Holborn.
A very good Tim Wisky with good harness.
A Chestnut Gelding, he goes safe. A good grey Mare and a well tempered Black boy who has recently had the smallpox.

BLACK HARRIOT:

After we were sold, I myself recall,
We were marched down
The cobbled quays where the ferrymen
Met us, the men with the moon faces.

CONSTANCE:

The men with the red sun faces.
Then we would be rowed to the waiting vessel.

17

FX:

(The sound of the wind with the sound of the sea.)

LAMPLIGHTER:

I can't tell you everything I lost. I lost my family. I lost my name.
I lost my country. I lost my freedom. I lost my weight.
I lost my sense of smell.

BLACK HARRIOT:

I lost my bearings. I lost faith
(for a while.)

CONSTANCE:

I lost my words.
I lost my tongue.

BLACK HARRIOT:

I lost my sense of fun.

LAMPLIGHTER:

At night... At night,

BLACK HARRIOT:

In the morning

MARY:

During the day

LAMPLIGHTER:

The men with the red sun faces came.
Nobody told my story before.
This is Me talking.

MARY:

This is Herself.

CONSTANCE:

This is Herself Talking.

LAMPLIGHTER:

I was the one who was stowed away.
For weeks on the *Mary*, the ship
Roared and tossed and everything was green.
Nobody knows what I went through coming here.
Just to stay alive, to see, to hear, to touch, to taste, to feel.
Nobody ever did stop and think about me. And so, my inside-
Voice got louder. And so my inside-thoughts got faster. And so
My outside-smile, wider.
And I learnt how to, how not to

CONSTANCE:

How to, how not to, what to not do, what to do, what not to do.

LAMPLIGHTER:

And I just about survived. I lived to tell this story.
I have forgotten what I have not remembered.
I am jumbled with the span of years, and the weight of things.
The weight of a horse bit in my mouth.

BLACK HARRIOT:

The weight of a chain on my arm.

MARY:

The weight of my body
On the scales before I was sold.

CONSTANCE:

The weight of my heavy heart.

MACBEAN:

I'll never forget the sight of her,
Standing on the cobbles with the tears
Flowing down her face. I can see her still.
Like she is still standing there.
Like it was yesterday.

LAMPLIGHTER:
> Over the big span of years
> I span myself, time myself.
> Could say those years are one step in time.
> Could say they are nothing at all.
> Not long ago.

BLACK HARRIOT:
> Not long ago enough yet.

CONSTANCE:
> Not far away enough yet.

MARY:
> Not in the past yet.

LAMPLIGHTER:
> Not as long ago as I would like to think.
> I can still stretch my arms back and be able to touch it again,
> smell it again, taste it again. Slavery. The feel of it.
> Don't forget to remember me. My voice is coming back.

MARY (*low*):
> This is Herself talking.

LAMPLIGHTER:
> My voice is coming back,
> Stronger by the day,
> By the light of the silvery moon.
> Close, slavery. Close – too close ever for comfort. A trudge and
> A slide away. A scrape and a pull away. A skip and a jump away.
> I remember when I was bought and sold and weighed as if it
> was yesterday.

BLACK HARRIOT:
> This is the story of Herself.

MARY:
> Told without the bit between the teeth.

LAMPLIGHTER:

The deaths I managed to avoid. The deaths
I did not live.

BLACK HARRIOT:

The endless deaths in us, the windowless deaths,
The deaths in the dungeons,
The deaths at sea
The deaths in the ship
The deaths in the new land
The deaths tied to the tree
The deaths in the plantation
The deaths in the shacks
The tobacco deaths, the sugar deaths.
The broken-hearted deaths. The love-missed and missing
Deaths. The in-your-face deaths. The stowed away deaths.
The sea deaths. The deaths at sea.

LAMPLIGHTER:

Death looked like a big steel ship called
Grace of God. Death tasted
Like a wounded bird, like captured freedom.

MARY:

And death was in all of us.

Scene 5: Shipping News

MACBEAN:

New Low, moving rapidly North-east and deepening.
Occasionally moderate or poor.
Buryed two slaves –
A man (no 140) and a boy (no 170)
Of the gravel and stoppage of urine.
A boy, no 158, then a girl no 172.
No 2 died of a flux. No 36 died of a flux.
Decreasing 4 for a time.
Biscay. Southwesterly veering westerly. Very rough or High.

LAMPLIGHTER:

Very rough or High.

MACBEAN:

Sole Lundy Fastnet Irish Sea

CONSTANCE:

Sole Lundy Fastnet Irish Sea, Sole Lonely Lundy, Fastnet,
Chain, Irish Sea. Monday, Monday. Tuesday, Tuesday. Fast.
Net. Sea. Fish. Soul. Sea.

MACBEAN:

From fore to aft
From the nose of the ship to the rudder
From shoulder to shoulder
Head to toe and toe to head,
The slaves were packed tight.

BLACK HARRIOT:

Dire was the tossing. Deep the moans.

CONSTANCE:

The men with the moon faces
Came to the shore
In big ships glinting like knives
Across the huge- big mirror water

LAMPLIGHTER:

I would rather die on yonder
Gallows than live in slavery

MACBEAN:

Squally showers for a time later.
1716. The *Windsor* reached Buenos Aires
with only 164 slaves surviving.
1714 The *Norman* left London
to pick up 300 slaves.
The *Norman* carried 150 gallons of malt,
Three hundred weight and ten pounds of flour.
12 hundredweight of biscuits. Coming soon.
Fifty chests of corn.
Twenty gallons of rum.

MARY:

Coming soon.

MACBEAN:

Rain later, moderate or good.

CONSTANCE:

Bad or good. Happy or sad. Big or small. Good or bad.
Sad or happy. Small or big.
Left or right. Right or wrong.

Scene 6: The Story Coming Back

FX:

(Exterior a place of memories: West African village. The sounds of children playing.)

LAMPLIGHTER:

I remember back before –
when I played with my friends in my
own country, and time was long
And trees were tall, I remember how my brother
and I watched out for kidnappers.
And how good my father was shaping the wood and metal, and
visits to the snake spirit, how some healers could really heal.
I remember how the Crocodile River,
ran fast. I remember my brother ran fast.
I remember our home with its cone-shaped roof, how my
brother and I belonged to our entire village. I remember the
days I lived before I came here, the life before.
The life before, the life I lived,
the life when I could breathe,
when I could smell the smells
and taste the tastes.

FX:

(Fade West African village. Cane field. Suggested rather than stated.)

LAMPLIGHTER:

Seems another me
lived that blessed life, another girl-
girl, deep in the interior country
far away from the coast,
a girl who had never ever seen the sea,
a girl who climbed to the top of trees.
I like to think she is up there, still,
mysterious, magical girl,
that she would never ever
hear this story.

MARY:

I wanted to run from that story.

CONSTANCE:

I wanted to pretend it never happened.

BLACK HARRIOT:

I wanted a break.

LAMPLIGHTER:

But no matter how fast I ran from my story,
No matter how many years,
The story just kept coming in and coming back
Like the sea to the shore
Like the sea always comes back to the shore.

BLACK HARRIOT:

Nobody told my story before.
You better listen good, girl.
Or I'm going to tell it twice!

MARY:

I wanted to be still and quiet.
Never to tell it.
When I lived it
sun up to sun set.

BLACK HARRIOT:

I was bought up on the Guinea Coast

CONSTANCE:

Imagine how much gold they took
To name a Coast after it.

MARY:

Imagine how much ivory

CONSTANCE:

To call a Coast Ivory Coast.

BLACK HARRIOT:
　　Imagine how many slaves

MARY:
　　To name a Coast Slave Coast?

CONSTANCE:
　　On the front of the 22-carat gold Guinea
　　There is an elephant and a castle,
　　Beneath the effigy of a right-facing King.

MACBEAN:
　　'Elephant and Castle' – very popular name for British pubs.

BLACK HARRIOT:
　　I was brought up on the Guinea Coast
　　When I was a young girl.
　　I was taken to St Kitts and sold
　　To Big Fat Planter
　　When I was a young girl.
　　I had two children
　　Their father was Big Fat Planter
　　When I was a young girl.

FX:
　　(Urban landscape. Suggested rather than stated.)

BLACK HARRIOT:
　　He brought us to England
　　When I was a young woman
　　Where he died of the smallpox
　　And left us all penniless
　　When I was a young woman.
　　Nothing else to do to stay alive

MARY:
　　When I was a young woman

BLACK HARRIOT:

I learnt to be a whore and I taught myself to read. I imagined a polite whore would fare better in the streets of London. Seventy of my regulars were Members of the House of Lords.

MARY:

When I was a young woman

CONSTANCE:

Lord, Lady, Sir, Master, Misses, Miss,
Yes, No. Yes Miss, No Miss. Yes Sir, No Sir.
Three bags full sir.
Young Missy-Missy said I must always
Answer yes or no if asked a question. I asked her what must I say if it is something I do not know. She answered why you must say you do not know of course.

BLACK HARRIOT:

Bien sur!

CONSTANCE:

Of course!

FX:

(Cane field.)

LAMPLIGHTER:

After the savage ship
There were the savage fields

MARY:

I was a field hand.
We made the fields; before us there were no fields;
We hacked back at the frontier wilderness,
Clinging to the edge
Of the wild frontier,
Slowly, painfully, pushing
Forward
And back.

We did the digging and the planting,
The cutting and the burning,
The carrying and the loading.

LAMPLIGHTER:

With hoes and knives and axes,
We sliced and stripped methodically,
Pushing back the line of cane,
We sweated and dripped continually.

MARY:

I worked in the Third Gang first,
Before the Second and then the first.
My work was heavy –
With the other women
I moved my hoes quick, quick and in time,
Singing to stop me dying in the sugar cane.
I could hear the sugarbirds whistling
In the sugar cane.

MUSIC:

(Sugar cane music.)

MARY:

From sun up to sun down
From four in the morning
Up with the conch shell

CONSTANCE:

Stripping it down, cutting it down.
Weeping sugar cane. Crying sugar cane.

MARY:

The sun told the time.
I was a field hand a long time
Third Gang, Second Gang, First
I worked the sugar cane.
My body never grew a child.
I was barren.

The child I might have had
Shrivelled up and died inside,
All the sugar sucked out of it.
I worked from when I was a girl
Till my old age.
Till my hands were wrinkled
Till my fingers looked like bindweed,
Knarled and crossed over themselves,
Like the roots of old trees.
I was a field hand all my days.

CONSTANCE:
I was a hand in the house

BLACK HARRIOT:
I was a hand in the street

LAMPLIGHTER:
I was a kitchen hand

BLACK HARRIOT:
My children, the BigHouseMan's children
Became servants to their brothers
And sisters. Their father
took us wherever he found us

MARY:
In the fields

BLACK HARRIOT:
In the house

CONSTANCE:
In the outhouse

MARY:

In his bedroom, kitchen. He noted it down in Latin. Every one of us he took, he wrote it in an old book.

CONSTANCE:

Tup – twice. Sup lect – on the bed; Sup Terr – On the ground. In Silva – in the woods. In Mag or in Parv – in great or small house. Illa habet menses – she has her period.

MACBEAN:

A slave was catched by Port Royal eating canes. Gave him a moderate whipping, pickled him well, made Hector shit in his mouth, immediately put a gag on whilst his mouth was full and made him wear it for five or six hours.

MARY:

He came for me night after night
Morning after morning.
Each time he left
He took a piece of me away.
I would be as silent as the moon.
One night when the moon was hidden
Behind the cloud, I hit him.
I hit him and hit him again.
Across the back of the head,
Hard as I could.
And as I did it I let out a roar.
It was not a scream. It was not a cry.

MACBEAN:

Slave Code: Under British law, if any slave resist his master, or owner, or other person, by his or her order, correcting such slave, and shall happen to be killed in such correction, it shall not be accounted felony; but the master, owner, and every such other person so giving correction, shall be free and acquit of all punishment and accusation for the same, as if such accident had never happened.

MARY:

He had me flogged then tied to the cherry tree and left for dead
I was left swinging for three days
To be seen, to break the spirit
Of anyone whose spirit might
Need breaking,

And after three days, I was cut down,
Expected to be dead. I was alive, just.
Still slightly breathing.
I was so beaten and whipped
That my face, back, hands were scarred.
I was ugly, knarled, twisted.
When I found myself alive
I knew I had been born again
And that the Lord Christ himself
Had come to give me salvation.

CONSTANCE:

Rise, let us be going; behold he is at hand that doth betray me.
Hereafter shall ye see the Son of man sitting on the right hand
of power and coming in the clouds of heaven.

ALL:

Amen!

CONSTANCE:

One teardrop, two, three teardrops, four, five teardrops, six,
seven teardrops, more, eight, nine, ten. Nine maidens crying,
eight, seven maidens sleeping, late, six maidens dying, five
maidens weeping, four maidens leaping, three, two, one, nought,
nothing. No. Stop. Stop. Stop.

LAMPLIGHTER:

I rose before dawn in that house and went to bed long after dusk.
I never knew a day off. The House Lady tried to teach me the
precepts of God's word. Thou shalt love thy neighbour as thyself.
But I was her slave.
I suppose she never saw me as her neighbour.

BLACK HARRIOT:
> She never saw me at all!

LAMPLIGHTER:
> Except when I did something she didn't like!
> She was always telling me I was lazy!

CONSTANCE:
> Visible. Invisible. See. Be not Seen. Hear be not heard.
> To be seen and not heard.
> To be or not to be, that is the Question.

MUSIC:
> *(The beat of a drum.)*

BLACK HARRIOT:
> When I arrived off the ship,
> I was polished with palm oil
> To make my dusty skin shine.
> My anus was plugged with wadding.

MARY:
> To fetch the best price for me.

LAMPLIGHTER:
> A note was placed OVER my head

MACBEAN:
> Good breeding stock

ALL:
> To fetch the best price for me.

The women start shouting and we hear a terrifying and sudden din and clamour. The yard door opening and the chorus shouts out prices (improvise).

LAMPLIGHTER:
> And without a moment's notice
> There was all hell and noise and scramble

And men rushing towards us
Wanting to buy us, turning us roughly round,

MARY:

Rushing towards us

BLACK HARRIOT:

Whirling us round

CONSTANCE:

Torn, yanked, pulled, pushed, kicked, stamped, branded.
I was given a new name.

MARY:

Mary MacDonald

CONSTANCE:

Constance

BLACK HARRIOT:

Black Harriot

MARY:

Mary MacDonald.
Original meaning uncertain.
Possibly, bitter or wished for child.

CONSTANCE:

I was named Constance.
Constance so that I would behave myself
So that I would be a virtue
Like my sisters Faith, Patience and Charity
So that in my abstraction
I would forever be constant.
Standing right there
At the side of, but not seen by,
In the house of, but not heard by,
In the bed of, but not loved by,
To be touched by, but not loved by,

To be felt by, but not loved by,
To always be, to never stop,
To always be Constant – reliable,
Sturdy, neger wench!

BLACK HARRIOT *is surprised at this and laughs out loud.*

BLACK HARRIOT:
I had a few names before this one.
My name is a joke.
There was a white Harriot once,
Not me.
They called me Black Harriot
So that white Harriot
Never needed to be called
White Harriot
And could just be Harriot.

CONSTANCE:
The old German for home ruler!

BLACK HARRIOT *laughs even more.*

BLACK HARRIOT:
Black Harriot

CONSTANCE:
Constance

MARY:
Mary MacDonald

BLACK HARRIOT:
We call her the Lamplighter.

LAMPLIGHTER:
They call me Lamplighter.

ANNIWAA:

    My name is Anniwaa

LAMPLIGHTER:

    There are things I can't help but remember.

ANNIWAA:

    Remember my name is Anniwaa.

LAMPLIGHTER:

    There are things I wish I could forget.

ANNIWAA:

    Don't forget my name is Anniwaa.

LAMPLIGHTER:

    These are the things I cannot stop remembering;
    these are the things I cannot stop forgetting.

MARY:

    I tell my story to remember.

BLACK HARRIOT:

    I tell my story to forget.

CONSTANCE:

    The History of the Lamplighter,
    related by Herself.

MARY:

    This is slavery.

FX:

    (The sound of sea on cobbles in the background.)

LAMPLIGHTER:

    I was stood on the cobbles outside the Inn in Avon,
    not so very long ago.
    My face was raining.

CONSTANCE:

I tell the story to let me sleep.

BLACK HARRIOT:

I tell the story to keep me awake.

CONSTANCE:

I tell the story to pass it on.

MARY:

I tell the story so the story will stop.

FX:

(Fade sea on cobbles.)

LAMPLIGHTER:

What I tell is not a story:
How they hid me in a sack,
How I thought I was going to be killed
Or eaten;
How I saw the furnace copper boiling.
How I smelt the blood on the galley.
How I heard the cries of women and children.
How I hit rock bottom.
My mouth was stuffed with rice, to drown my crying,
How I felt like jumping ship.
I never saw my brother again.
I never smelt the smell of my own country.
I never heard my mother's voice again.
I never did not feel like jumping ship.

BLACK HARRIOT:

After the floating prison
There was the field prison
After the field prison
There was the kitchen prison.
Anything I did, or said
Was wrong, always wrong

CONSTANCE:

    The whip was made out of plaited cow skin.
    It could take the skin
    Off horses' backs or lay marks
    In a deal board;
    When I was being flogged for nothing
    I never did cry out or scream
    I stayed silent – close to serene,
    I would not give the mistress
    the satisfaction of my distress.

LAMPLIGHTER:

    And I heard The HouseLady one day say
    When she was teaching me the book,
    All things whatsoever ye would that men should do to you,
    do you even so to them;
    For this is the law of the prophets.

CONSTANCE:

    When I was moved from the field
    To the house, I thought I'd got lucky.
    But The HouseLady was as demanding
    As any field driver.
    HouseLady would lie in bed till noon
    While I looked after her children.
    Her children talk my talk
    And walk my walk
    And know me better than their mother.
    Those children know my songs

SONG:

    (Spiritual: the next part the chorus sings.)

SONG:

    (CONSTANCE sings a Creole lullaby under the others singing Daniel.)

ALL:

    I'm gonna tell my Lord Daniel

I'm gonna tell my Lord Daniel

How you done me here Daniel

How you done me here Daniel

This aint none of my home Daniel

This aint none of my home Daniel

Slip and slide the street Daniel

Slip and slide the street Daniel.

Didn't my Lord Deliver Daniel

Didn't my Lord Deliver Daniel

Didn't my Lord Deliver Daniel

And why not every man

MARY:
In Jamaica, I worked hard.

CONSTANCE:
In St Lucia, I worked hard.

BLACK HARRIOT:
In St Kitts, I worked hard.

CONSTANCE:
Spinning and weaving and making clothes,

MARY:
Digging and planting, cutting and burning.
Water had to be carried from the wells and pumps
Heavy backbreaking loads carried for miles.

CONSTANCE:

I was plucked from the fields and trained in the house. On call twenty-four hours a day, seven days a week; to her, to him, to them. Used until I was sixteen and then sold again.

MACBEAN:

A neger Wench fit for plantation work, or very capable of making a Good House Wench having for some months served as such in a family.

CONSTANCE:

And in that house, the planters offered me
To their friends for sexual favours,
To neighbours, to young men.

MACBEAN:

A neger wench I have must be brought to Knowledge.

CONSTANCE:

I could tell HouseLady didn't like it
When Fatman did what he did to me.
Next day, she'd punish me for
His punishing ways.
By the break of day, I was broken.
By the close of day, I was broken.

CONSTANCE:

This story was repeated.

LAMPLIGHTER:

This story was repeated in the sugar mills.

BLACK HARRIOT:

This story was repeated in the tobacco fields.

LAMPLIGHTER:

This is the story of the Lamplighter.

MARY:

Related by Herself.

SONG:

(The next part is sung.)

BLACK HARRIOT:

Ah well looka here missy, what in the worl' are you trying to do.

CONSTANCE:

I said looka here missy, what in the worl' are you tryin' a do.

LAMPLIGHTER:

Don' know what makes me love you, you gonna break my heart in two.
(Repeat song twice.)

CONSTANCE:

I was picked from the fields to work
In the house: I learned: sewing, spinning, steaming, boiling, hot.
Wiping, cleaning, polishing, spick and span.
The Man can have you anytime he can.
Shimmy shammy. Hand on foot. Rub a dub.
Three men in a tub. Shimmy shammy. Mammy.
Mammy. Mammy. Filthy, dirty. Dirty, dirty, clean.

BLACK HARRIOT:

A lick and a promise.

MARY:

I was always at the field driver's beck and call.

BLACK HARRIOT:

I wouldn't let them take me. I took them.
I grabbed their balls and pulled them.
I licked their faces. I rode them like
I was wild on a wild horse, *Yahoooooo!*
I took him and took him and took him again!
Till his red face got redder,

40

His red chest got weaker.
I knocked the breath out his chest
And he was panting like there
Was never going be any tomorrow.
I took him for everything he got.
I took him till I finished him off.

CONSTANCE *roars with laughter.*

MACBEAN:

Thomas Sutherland made free with the slave women. He used to say that a likely negur wench was fit to be a Queen. It is not known how many queens he fitted into his plantation. He was a gentleman greatly addicted to his women slaves.

SONG:

(The next part is sung.)

LAMPLIGHTER:

The rich man comes from down below

CHORUS:

Yo ho, yo ho

LAMPLIGHTER:

What he comes for I guess I know

CHORUS:

Long time ago

LAMPLIGHTER:

He comes to take his slave girl

CHORUS:

Yo ho, yo ho

LAMPLIGHTER:

The mistress pretend she don't know

CHORUS:
Long time ago.

FX:
(Quay.)

MARY:
She stood on those cobbles and was sold for eighty pounds.
She was sold to the plantation.
We call her The Lamplighter.

LAMPLIGHTER:
I imagined I could see light on water,
A tall house with light
Guiding me to shore

CONSTANCE:
I imagined one day I would find my daughter,
A small girl,
With dark curly hair.

LAMPLIGHTER:
I carried the light from the day
You lost her.
A bright light across the deep dark sea.

CONSTANCE:
I carried a light for my sons, my daughters. One day
I'd find the wings to fly away.

LAMPLIGHTER:
I carried the light to light the lamps
The lamps across the wide dark sea

CONSTANCE:
I carried the lamp inside me,
And it was glowing deeply

LAMPLIGHTER:

    I never did ever part
    With that constant flame
    Not even when they broke my heart.

CONSTANCE:

    I protected it from wind and rain;
    I'd see my children one more time.

LAMPLIGHTER:

    They call me the Lamplighter.
    They call me the Lamplighter.

Scene 7: Shipping News

MACBEAN:

The weather, still dirty.
Buryed a boy slave of the flux.
Buryed a man slave of the flux.
The general synopsis at Midday Atlantic –
Low 967. The *Dorothy*. The *Windsor*.
Coming soon.

MARY:

Tobacco, sugar – coming soon.

BLACK HARRIOT:

The British sweet tooth – coming soon.
Hot puddings, cold puddings, steamed puddings, baked puddings,
pies, tarts, coming soon. Moderate or good. Creams, moulds,
charlottes, bettys, trifles, fools. Coming soon.

MACBEAN:

Buryed a man slave. Buryed a boy.
Buyed a boy slave of the flux.

LAMPLIGHTER:

Into the shark infested Atlantic,
The black deaths slipped. The sharks
Followed the slave ships for the pickings.
And the seagulls that carried the souls
Of the dead sailors flew over the dead.

MACBEAN:

The right hand and foot of one
Across the head and foot of the other
So that they are fettered together
And cannot move either hand or foot.
From head to toe and toe to foot.

Two days before docking in
The slave galley could be smelled,
The putrescence of blood, faeces, vomit and rotting bodies,
Wafting downwind,
The smell of the dead carried
Across the water to the Port.
Permanent trade winds blow
From the Northeast and East
Across the Atlantic.

BLACK HARRIOT:

Dire is the tossing. Deep the moans.

MACBEAN:

Buryed a woman slave of the flux.
No 29. Buryed a girl slave. No 74.
Later Decreasing Four or Five.

CONSTANCE:

The slavers followed the sugar.
The sharks followed the slave ships.
The slaves' bones sunk to the bottom of the sea.

LAMPLIGHTER:

I would rather die on yonder gallows
Than live in slavery.

BLACK HARRIOT:

Demerara. Muscovada.
Molasses. Treacle. Syrup.
Brown sugar. White sugar. Moist sugar.
Castor sugar, raw sugar.

Scene 8: Sugar

FX:

(During the scene we hear the sound of sugar cane being cut and the sound of a sugar mill.)

MARY:

Mrs Hannah Glasse's first cookery book in England. *The Art of Cookery made plain and easy.*

BLACK HARRIOT:

Take three quarters of a pound of best moist sugar to make a cake the Spanish way.

CONSTANCE:

Rum had a wonderful history of success in Britain, so did jam. La dolce vita!

BLACK HARRIOT:

This is the dawning of the Age of Sugar.

LAMPLIGHTER:

My story is the story of sugar.

MACBEAN:

The owner of Worthy Park, Jamaica declared, 'The white man cannot labour under a burning sun without certain death, though the Negro can in all climates with impunity.'

LAMPLIGHTER:

My story is the story of sugar.
My story is not sweet.

MACBEAN:

The careful benevolence of providence has provided the Negroes with thick skins.

MARY:

I carried manure in baskets, weighing eighty pounds, on my head. The holes dug for the cane were deep and wide.

LAMPLIGHTER:

The sun baked the heavy soils.
The sun baked my skin.
The cakes were baked. The cakes were baking. The cakes had been baked. The cakes will be baked.

BLACK HARRIOT:

Pound cake! A pound of floor. A pound of butter. A pound of sugar. One dozen eggs.

MARY:

The cut cane was heavy and cumbersome.

CONSTANCE:

20 tons of cane to produce one ton of sugar.

MARY:

At Worthy Park, 89 of the 133 field slaves were women.

LAMPLIGHTER:

We did the planting, cutting, burning, carrying, loading, slicing and stripping.

MACBEAN:

The long sweep of Jamaica's fertile southern coast was pitted with plantations.

MARY:

I was always hungry. I never stopped being hungry especially in the summer. We got breakfast at nine when we'd been up since four. When the belly is hollow, when the ground feels like it is moving up to meet you, when the emptiness inside you is like something moving. You are all the time imagining food.

LAMPLIGHTER:

> One time I run away
> Crawling through the tall sugar cane
> Watching out for snakes
> I get as far as the forest in the hills.
> Dogs are sent after me.
> When the people catch me
> They flog me
> Till my back is so crisscross
> It looks like cut cane

MACBEAN:

> The posterior is made bare and the offender is extended prone on the ground. The driver, with his long and heavy whip, inflicts the lashes under the eye of the overseer.

LAMPLIGHTER:

> My story is the story of sugar.

BLACK HARRIOT:

> In 1775 the British West Indies Colonies produces 100,000 tons of sugar

CONSTANCE:

> Syllabubs and fancys, junkets and ices, milk puddings, suet puddings.

LAMPLIGHTER:

> I cut the cane. After I cut the cane, the cane is crushed in the sugar mills and processed in the noisy factories and boiling houses.

MACBEAN:

> As we pass along the shore, the Plantations appear to us one above the other like several stories in stately buildings which afforded us a large proportion of delight.

BLACK HARRIOT:
>My story is the story of sugar.
>I was stolen for sugar.
>I gave my body up for sugar.
>I nearly died for sugar.
>Sugar is my family tree.
>I have no sugar daddy.

CONSTANCE:
>They took my little girl
>when she was three years old
>already old enough to be my soul
>mate, to shadow me in the sun
>all day and ask a hundred whys.
>I never told her lies.
>I never talk about her.
>They took her and they sold her.
>One, two.

MACBEAN:
>A three-year-old girl is to be sold
>Betwixt the hours of six and eight
>In Bristol coffee house, sturdy, healthy, has had the small pox,
>for five shillings.

CONSTANCE:
>I remember when she was in my belly
>counting the months
>– one two three –
>and trying to imagine her
>and trying to think how
>if she were a girl
>– four five six –
>I could make her look ugly
>enough when she got older
>– nine ten eleven –
>so that none of them ever came near her
>on the day they sold her,

my body shook and shook so much
that my speech went.
For months, I couldn't say a word.
How many moons ago
how many years
– twelve thirteen fourteen fifteen –
since I seen my four children?
My baby boy, my wise girl
with the big questions, my big boy
whose eyes changed the time
he saw me being beaten?
How many moons since I saw my children?

MACBEAN:

The rule of thumb on the sugar plantations:
One slave required for every acre of land.

BLACK HARRIOT:

Jamaica produced nearly a quarter of the world's sugar.

MARY:

Back in the big house,
The BigMan entertained his friends.

MACBEAN:

Wednesday, 15 March 1775. John Cope, Richard Vassall, William
Blake Esqr dined with me and stayed till nine in the evening.
Mr Cope stayed all night. Had mutton broth, roast mutton and
broccoli, carrots and asparagus, stewed mudfish, roast goose and
paw paw, apple sauce, stewed giblets, some fine lettuce which Mr
Vassall brought me, crabs, cheese, mush melon. Punch, porter,
ale, cider, Madeira wine and brandy.

LAMPLIGHTER:

I was his cook for many years.
If I ever made a mistake,
If they ever thought I could have done something better.
Nobody said anything to me. I was stripped directly and they
cut away at me.

I was whipped so many times,
My back was all corruption, as if it would rot. After the lashes
They'd wash my back with salt water,
Rub it with rags, and then send me straight back to work again
in the kitchen.

BLACK HARRIOT:

Syllabubs and fancys, junkets and ices, milk puddings, suet pud-
dings.

MUSIC:

(Sugar cane music, the next part is sung.)

SONG:

(Spiritual.)

ALL:

Go down, Moses, way down in Egypt's land
Tell old Pharoah, Let my people go.

BLACK HARRIOT:

Go down Moses

MARY:

way down Egypt's land

CONSTANCE:

Tell old Pharoah,

ALL:

Let my people go.

LAMPLIGHTER:

I stood on the cobbled quay,
And was resold to the Plantations.
I left Avonmouth
And crossed the Atlantic.
This is my story.

MARY:

    Narrated by herself.

LAMPLIGHTER:

    I was shy of my story for years.
    I did the thing that you are taught to do.

ALL:

    SSSSSSSSSSSSSSSSSSSSSSSssssssssssssssshhhhhhhhhhhhhhhh-
    hhhhhhhhhhhhhhhhhhhhhhhh

CONSTANCE + ALL:

    Keep it quiet. Button it. Bite your lip. Bite your tongue. Pipe
    down. Cut the cackle. Stow it. Mum's the word. Whist! Hush.
    Hold your tongue! Keep your mouth shut! Shut it. Keep sch-
    tum!

MARY *(softly)*:

    Hush now. Don't explain. There, there. Hush now.

LAMPLIGHTER *(sings)*:

    Hush little baby, don't you cry,
    Mama's going to sing you a lullaby.

CONSTANCE:

    The field driver comes for me early. He is coming for me because
    he is coming for her. She won't go anywhere without me. She is
    Only three. She is a girl who says things that always surprise.
    The other day she ask me if she will be a man or a woman when
    she grow up?

    It is already hot. Her hand sticks to me like we are joined to-
    gether. I squeeze her hand. I always tell her that is me passing
    my love to her – our special hand squeeze. She squeezes back.
    It is her reply. She loves that. How the love happens without
    words.
    I know, as I walk up the hill, along the side of the sugar cane
    past the orchard, towards the Big House; I know, as I look down
    to the ground, wanting for the ground to open up and swallow

us both up; I know, as I walk with her little hand in mine, that I will never forget the feel of it, slightly sticky, warm, small fingers. There is nothing like the feeling of a small child's hand in yours. You are the guide. It is full of faith, light, trusting. Sometimes, she likes to close her eyes and for me to lead her. Sometimes she likes me to tell her life by reading the darker lines on her hand, the lifelines. I tell her she will grow into an old woman; she has a strong heart. She will have five children. I like to count my child's children.

One, two, three, four, five.

(As if she is hiding in numbers.)

LAMPLIGHTER:

Hush sssssshhhhhhhhhhhhh.

Scene 9: Shipping News

MACBEAN:
Across the green sea of darkness sailed

CONSTANCE:
The *Brookes*, the *Vigilant*, the *Iphigenia*.

MACBEAN:
Galeforce ten. Rough or High.
120 slaves sailed on the *Royal Charlotte*
– fifty died.
105 slaves sailed on the *Molly*
– fifty died.

MUSIC:
(A death roll.)

MACBEAN:
6th September 1781, the Zong was on its
Well-tried route from Liverpool, to
West Africa, and on to the Caribbean.
Ship's Captain, Luke Collingwood,
Decided to jettison live slaves into
The sea, so that he could claim
Insurance on each life.

CONSTANCE:
£30 per dead slave.

MACBEAN:
29 November, the first batch –
54 slaves thrown overboard alive.
A day later 42 living slaves
Thrown to the sharks.
On the third day,
26 more slaves thrown to sea.
On the third day,

The slaves put up a fight, and were
Shackled before they were drowned
In the early, unmarked, grave of the sea.

BLACK HARRIOT:
Ten people saw what was happening
And refused to hang around waiting.
They jumped, up high,
They dived down into the sea.
Those were the deaths with wings,
Like songs, like freedom songs,
Rising up and out at last.
No more no more, no more, no more.

MACBEAN:
Across the roaring Atlantic tossed
The steel-stowed, stocked slave-ships

BLACK HARRIOT:
Tobacco for the pipes of Englishmen.
Coffee for fashionable society.
Sugar for the English poor.

Scene 10: Death – free at last

FX:

(Cane field.)

MARY:

Clarissa was Congolese, was thirteen
By a guess,
She was ill when she arrived and they
Put her to work on the second Gang
And changed her name to Prattle.

LAMPLIGHTER:

I remember. I forget.

MARY:

At seventeen, she succumbed to the flux and died.

BLACK HARRIOT:

Raveface was 24 at a guess
When she arrived
She was a field hand for forty years.
Freedom finally came for Raveface
In 1838. She was 64.

LAMPLIGHTER:

I remember. I forget.

CONSTANCE:

Phoebe, a Coromantee, suffered from Yaws.

MACBEAN:

It is nauseous and loathsome in appearance. Its frightful ravages, its twitching pains, extending to the very marrow, bring with it a deformity of bone and flesh that is horrifying.

LAMPLIGHTER:

So many of the field hands
Had crab yaws on their hands
Or ringworms on the side of their necks.

BLACK HARRIOT:

Cure for Yaws. Stand them in a cask where there is a little fire
in a pot. Give them a mixture of two woods, Bois Royale and
Bois Fer and apply an ointment of limejuice and rust of iron to
the sores.

LAMPLIGHTER:

This is my story.
Told by myself.
I am dead and alive.
I am wanted, dead or alive.

SONG:

O Canaan, sweet Canaan
I am bound for the land of Canaan.

O Canaan, sweet Canaan
I am bound for the land of Canaan

O Canaan, sweet Canaan
I am bound for the land of Canaan

I am going to the promised land
I am going to the promised land.

LAMPLIGHTER:

And when one of us died a sugar death,
Of Yaws or dysentery or heat
When one of us died
Of leprosy, TB, pneumonia or yellow fever,
When one of us died because
We couldn't take no more
Out in the sugar fields

When one of us died again
Out in the tobacco fields
We would call out her name.

ALL:

Clarissa, Phoebe, Raveface, Sally.

LAMPLIGHTER:

And into her grave would go, quick, quick,
Some rum,
Some rum and some casava bread,
Even when we're hungry, hurry up,
No time now, no time to mourn the dead,
A pipe, quickly now,
A pipe and a tier to light the pipe.

CONSTANCE:

I will not forget her!

ALL:

Clarissa, Phoebe, Raveface, Sally.

LAMPLIGHTER:

Free at last! Free at last!
Thank God Almighty, she's free at last.

ALL:

Clarissa, Phoebe, Raveface, Sally

CONSTANCE:

I remember Sally!

BLACK HARRIOT:

Was always running away
She was say, seventeen
Or eighteen years old,
She was Congolese.
Chains and stocks did not stop her.

MARY:

Remember Mountain Lucy? Mountain Lucy
miscarried after she drank Contra Yerva every day
on purpose. Remember.

CONSTANCE:

I remember Mountain Lucy!

ALL:

Clarissa, Phoebe, Raveface, Sally, Mountain Lucy.

LAMPLIGHTER:

Thank God Almighty! Free at last!

SONG:

(The next part should be sung by the chorus each sharing the lines.)

ALL *(singing)*:

Dark down there in the faceless dark
We couldn't see for looking
We couldn't take your hand down there
We couldn't hear for listening.

Remember the steps down
We couldn't take for breaking
We couldn't breathe down there in the dark
We couldn't speak for fearing.

Then, up we came two at a time
We couldn't walk for running
Up and out along a strange new path
We couldn't stop for going.

CONSTANCE:

I walk along the path with my bean girl's hand in mine. 'Bring
her up to the House. Make her look nice.' Maybe I am wrong
and this day will not be an end. Maybe I will walk back down
the hill with my little bean girl's hand in mine.

I know if I try and run, or if I try and get her to run, we will both be dead. He is walking close behind. I try and blot him out, so that this last walk is our own. What is she wearing? What smile today? What questions?

I can't remember. I remember I smile as much as I can, so that if she ever remembers me, she will see that: us two walking, the sugar cane, the breeze, the special hand squeeze.

As I walk along that path, slow as I can, with her hand in mine, I try and figure which would be better the dead death, or the living one. Last night I placed my hand over her mouth and her nose. It could have been easy. But suppose I am wrong? Suppose I will be walking back down the hill with my bean girl's hand in mine?

The man behind pushes me – Hurry up there!
Move it! He says. Her eyes are big saucer shapes.
She says to me – Where are we going?
What do I say to her?
I make something up, I think.
I can't remember what foolish thing I think up at the time.
Anyway, whatever it is I say and said, she.
She believes me.
Why wouldn't she?

Scene 11: Runaway

FX:

(We hear the sound of running and bush being cut and the ominous beating of a drum. The barking of dogs. The firing of a gun.)

LAMPLIGHTER:

I am a fugitive. I have been running away since I was a little girl, since I was eleven, nearly twelve years old.

At first I could only run away in my dreams. Then, on the plantation I was shackled and watched. One visiting day, visiting another plantation, the shackles were off and their eyes weren't checking me. I ran. Away.

MACBEAN:

Any slave who escape beyond the River is to lose an ear and be branded with the letter R on the chin.

MARY:

Where can you run to? Only into the arms of Jesus.

LAMPLIGHTER:

I am running to my mama, she is wearing her yellow head tie.

ANNIWAA:

I am running to my mama, today she is wearing her yellow head tie.

LAMPLIGHTER:

She is the lamp that guides me.

ANNIWAA:

I have been running away since I was eleven, nearly twelve years old.

BLACK HARRIOT:

Villain, Trash, Whore and Strumpet
Frequently absconded
David, born to big Sue
Was always running away.
Strumpet was described as Field Able Runaway.
Lady ran way in 1785
Was caught in 88
And returned late
One dark night.

MACBEAN:

Who ever shall bring the said woman back, or give information
that she be back again, shall receive a handsome reward.

BLACK HARRIOT:

Where can the runaway hide my dear?
Where can the runaway hide?
In the middle of London, in Yorkshire
On the edges of a Jamaican plantation,
In the bush or in the mountains,
Where can the runaway hide, my dear?

MARY:

Where can the runaway hide.

BLACK HARRIOT:

In the forest or by the rivers,
In the swamp land or in the towns,
In the thicket, in the thick of it,
On another plantation,
Or with good friends –
Where can the runaway hide, my dear?

MARY:

Where can the runaway hide.

CONSTANCE:

>The runaway crossed the water
>The runaway crossed the sea
>The runaway was looking for her daughter
>The runaway was looking for her family.

BLACK HARRIOT:

>Where can the runaway hide, my dear?

MARY:

>Where can the runaway hide.

LAMPLIGHTER:

>When five Angolans ran away in 1761,
>They headed east for as long as they could,
>Thinking they would return to their own country,
>If they just stayed east.

BLACK HARRIOT:

>Running away was a leap in the dark.
>Running away was a search for the heart.

LAMPLIGHTER:

>Doll ran way to go a courting.
>Philippa ran off to go a sweet hearting.
>Clarissa ran to find her free mother,
>Living under the green trees in Roebuck.

BLACK HARRIOT:

>The Barbados Slave Code of 1661
>To the enslaved, it gives – no rights,
>No rights of man, no rights of woman,
>Not even the right to life.

CONSTANCE:

>Jamaica Slave Code, St Lucia Slave Code, Demerara Slave Code,
>Dominica Slave Code, St Vincent Slave Code, Tobago Slave Code.

LAMPLIGHTER:

In 1817, Chloe was trusted by the Houselady
To go and sell glassware.
She never came back.

MARY:

Jane Frances ran away and tried to pass
As a free women, and fled the island.

LAMPLIGHTER:

A few miles up the Savannah River
One hundred slaves lived free
And formed their own community.
They lived on corn, hogs and fowl.

BLACK HARRIOT:

Kate ran away in 1756,
She ran for thirty miles to West River.

MACBEAN:

It is enacted that baptism does not alter the condition to the
person as to his bondage or freedom.

MARY:

Hearken unto this, O Job, stand still, and consider the wondrous
works of God.

BLACK HARRIOT:

Joan had a smiling countenance.
Jack had a pleasant countenance.
Tom Buck had a tongue full of compliments.

MARY:

All three said sweet, honey words to the Man.
All three ran away.

CONSTANCE:

Fast as they can.

LAMPLIGHTER:

> I ran away five times.
> Four times they got me and brought me back.
> Even the forty lashes on my back,
> Even the hundred and forty,
> Didn't stop me trying again,
> Just to feel those moments
> Of freedom, to taste the air.
> But the fifth time, I made it!
> This is the story of how I got
> From here to there:
> This is the story of the Lamplighter.

MARY:

> Related by Herself!

MACBEAN:

> Lady Broughton of Marchwhiel Hall near Wrexham in 1686.

CONSTANCE:

> 'A guinea reward for the return of my black boy.'

LAMPLIGHTER:

> Colonel Kirke advertised for a sixteen year old runaway.

CONSTANCE:

> 'He has a silver Collar about his Neck, upon which is the Colonel's Coat of Arms and Cipher.'

MACBEAN:

> William, King of England from 1689 to 1702,
> Had a favourite black slave.
> The bust is on display at Hampton Court
> Complete with carved white marble collar
> With a padlock, like a dog's collar.

CONSTANCE:

> Hue and cry advertisements:

MARY:

Four guineas offered for a man called York owned by Betsey.
A boy of say twelve years, stocky, well-set,
Goes by the name of Somerset,
Is sought by his Master, Mr Ross,
Of Bristol.

CONSTANCE:

A guinea for his capture.

MACBEAN:

A black slave going by the name of Starling,
Who blows the French horn well,
Ran away from a publican in Princes Street.

BLACK HARRIOT:

Runaway runaway, country or town.
Runaway, runaway, don't slow down.
Runaway, runaway, girl or boy.
Runaway, runaway, freedom is joy.

CONSTANCE:

We reach the verandah. I want to sink into the floor and dis-
appear. I want to walk through the wall. I want to be able to
walk on water. I want to believe in God. Please God. If ever
there was a day, God, to make me believe in you, make it this
day. If ever there was a moment, God, to show me a sign of
you, give my sign right now.

It happens slow and then all of a sudden it happens fast. The
Man plucks my bean girl from me, forces his dirty fingers into
her mouth, rubs her gums and teeth.

MACBEAN:

Constance is 45 yrs of age, dark complexion, round built, intel-
ligent & genteel... She has been the mother of 15 children, 4 of
whom had been sold away from her, one is still held in Peters-
burg, the others are all dead. At the sale of one of her children

'she was thrown into such a state of grief that she lost speech for a month in consequence thereof, convulsions were very frequently brought on'.

CONSTANCE:

My light is gone. Every word I could say is gone. I am struck. I am falling down. I am falling still; my bean girl is three years old. She will always be three years old. I wonder if she will remember me. Or if she will forget.

LAMPLIGHTER *(whisper)*:

Remember, forget. Forget,
Remember. Remember, forget,
Forget, remember.

MARY:

Runaway runaway, country or town.
Runaway, runaway, don't slow down.
Runaway, runaway, girl or boy.
Runaway, runaway, freedom is joy.

LAMPLIGHTER:

When BigCheese told me that I was made for his use, made to obey his command in everything, that I was nothing but a slave whose will must be to surrender to his, never before had my puny arm felt so strong.

CONSTANCE:

I said to herself.

LAMPLIGHTER:

I swore to myself.

MARY:

I swore to herself.

LAMPLIGHTER:

One day I would be free.

Scene 12: Shipping News

CONSTANCE:

> Across the Atlantic, the slave ships sped –
> The *Ann*, the *Margery*, the *Diana*
> The *Angel*, the *Jesus*, the *Grace of God.*

MARY:

> The *Grace of God.*

BLACK HARRIOT:

> The *Blessing*, the *Bridget*, the *Fanny*, the *Hannah*,
> the *Reformation*, the *Perseverance.*

MARY:

> The *Perseverance.*

CONSTANCE:

> The *Charming Sally*, the *Ruby*, the *Hare*,
> The *Isabella*, the *Eliza*, the *Othello*,
> The *Sarah*, the *Ferret*, the *Rebecca.*

MACBEAN:

> Across the icy glare of water
> Across the never ending sea
> Far away from land and daughter
> Far away from family.

LAMPLIGHTER:

> Nothing to see but sea
> Nothing to hear but roar
> Nothing to smell but blood and gore
> Nothing to taste but salt and rice
> Nothing to sense but fear.

MACBEAN:

> January 1st Buried one man – of dysentery.
> January 3rd – one woman – ditto.

January 6th – one woman – of a lethargy.
January 15th – one boy of a dysentery.
January 16th – one manboy – ditto.
January 17th – one girl – ditto.
January 18th – one man – ditto.
January 19th – one boy – ditto.
January 28th – one boy – ditto.
January 31st – one woman – of sulkiness.

LAMPLIGHTER:

I would rather die on yonder gallows
Than live in slavery.

MACBEAN:

The moon that night was in a shroud.

CONSTANCE:

The moon was in a shroud.

MACBEAN:

The gales were high and the gales were loud.
One African in three did not survive the
Slave ships. One African in three did
Not survive the first three years in
Her or his new country.

MARY:

Ten million tons of sugar cane arrived.

BLACK HARRIOT:

Raw sugar. Moist sugar. White sugar. Brown sugar.
Muscovada. Molasses. Syrup. Treacle. Caramel.

CONSTANCE:

Coming soon. Sweet, not sour.

Scene 13: British Cities

FX:

(The sound of the sea at the port, the sound of ships arriving, cargo being unloaded. Noisily, bustly.)

*(*MACBEAN *in this part could experiment with the accents of the cities: Glasgow, Liverpool, Bristol, London.)*

(The women should speak fast in this section and overlap each other, to give a sense of the city being built, brick by brick, in words.)

LAMPLIGHTER:
Sea, city, harbour, port
Sugar city, sugar ship,
Tobacco city, tobacco lips.
My story is the story of the city.

ALL:
Boom! Boom! Boom!

CONSTANCE:
Liverpool, Bristol, London, Manchester, Lancaster, Glasgow

BLACK HARRIOT:
Brass!

LAMPLIGHTER:
Glassware!

MARY:
Banking!

BLACK HARRIOT:
Cotton, striped cotton, coloured cotton!

MARY:
Manufactured goods!

70

LAMPLIGHTER:
　　Canal expansion!

ALL:
　　Boom! Boom! Boom!

BLACK HARRIOT:
　　Banking!

MARY:
　　Ship building industry!

CONSTANCE:
　　Banking infrastructure!

MARY:
　　Guns, shackles.

ALL *(more sinisterly)*:
　　Boom! Boom!

LAMPLIGHTER:
　　Insurance!

CONSTANCE:
　　Investments from merchants!

MARY:
　　Timber, iron!

CONSTANCE:
　　Slave ships!

LAMPLIGHTER:
　　Houses, banks, buildings, businesses
　　Carriages, horses, cobbles, dresses.
　　In the night, the city grew.

ALL:

    Boom! Boom! Boom!

LAMPLIGHTER:

    By the morning there was another new

MARY:

    Pub, coffee house, bank, merchant's house,
    Art gallery, Customs house, Venturer's House.

MACBEAN:

    The Ship Building Industry. Shipping.

CONSTANCE:

    Ship bread, ship biscuit, ship breaker, slaver, ship broker, ship fever, ship store, slaver, ship cargo, ship stowage, stow away, ship rat, slaver, ship days.

MACBEAN:

    Ship: to put or take (person or things)
    Ship: to shoulder a burden

CONSTANCE:

    HardSHIP, WorkmanSHIP, WorSHIP, relationSHIP, authorSHIP! *(She sounds very excited.)* AuthorSHIP!

MACBEAN:

    The British System is the most gigantic system of slavery the world has yet seen.

BLACK HARRIOT:

    London, Birmingham, Manchester, Liverpool, Bristol,
    Glasgow, Edinburgh, Lancaster, Hull.

LAMPLIGHTER:

    I put those cities on the map.

SONG:

    (Folksong.)

MARY:

> Virginia Street, Tobago Street, Jamaica Street, Ingram Street, Glassford Street

MACBEAN:

> John Glassford, partner in Thistle Bank
> Owned twenty-five slave ships.
> His annual turnover was half a million sterling.

SONG:

> *(Folksong.)*

BLACK HARRIOT *(sings)*:

> I'm only a common old working slave.

SONG:

> *(Protest song.)*

ALL SING:

> *But the banks are made of marble*
> *With a guard at every door*
> *And the vaults are stuffed with silver*
> *That the people sweated for.*

CONSTANCE:

> Ten twenty thirty forty fifty sixty seventy eighty one hundred pounds, ten twenty thirty forty fifty sixty seventy eighty. Two hundred thousand pounds. *(And so on.)*

FX:

> *(We hear the sound of money being counted.)*

BLACK HARRIOT:

> Buchanan Street is my main shopping street, apart from Sauchiehall Street.
> That's where I get my bling!

MACBEAN:

Bishop Pococke visted Glasgow in 1760. He remarked, 'this city has above all others felt the advantages of the union in the West Indian trade which is very great especially in tobacco, indigoes and sugar'.

CONSTANCE:

I put that city on the map.

SONG:

I belong to Glasgow, dear old Glasgow town.
There's nothing the matter with Glasgow,
For it's going round and round.

BLACK HARRIOT:

The ships are being built, the buildings are going up, banks, shops, houses, bakers, pubs, coffee houses, streets, canals,

FX:

(We hear the sounds of port cities, foghorns, ships coming in, iron-works, etc.)

CONSTANCE:

Share prices going up! Up up up! Invest now!

MARY:

I am collapsing.

ANNIWAA:

Keep me company.

MACBEAN:

There is not a brick in this city but what is cemented with the blood of a slave.

CONSTANCE *(sings)*:

Glasgow belongs to me!

LAMPLIGHTER:
  My blood

MARY:
  My sweat

CONSTANCE:
  My tears

LAMPLIGHTER:
  In the first year of the

CONSTANCE:
  Quote

LAMPLIGHTER:
  Free

CONSTANCE:
  Unquote

LAMPLIGHTER:
  Trade.
  Bristol alone shipped 160,950 Africans to the sugar plantation.

CONSTANCE *(sings)*:
  Bristol Belongs to Me

MACBEAN:
  Bristolians depend for their subsistence on their West Indies
  and African Trade which employs great numbers of people in
  shipyards and in the manufacture of wool, iron, tin, copper,
  brass, etc.
  Fellow citizens of Bristol. Do not lay the axe at the root of your
  own prosperity by supporting the abolition of slavery!

FX:
  (Quay.)

LAMPLIGHTER:

I stood there on the cobbles,
At the Port in the pouring rain.
I couldn't believe it was
Happening all over again.
I was brought to England
From the Plantation,
I managed to run away.
I was hiding in the hole of a roof
When I heard a bell ringer calling out
For me

FX:

(We hear the bells ringing.)

MACBEAN:

Guinea reward for black girl!

LAMPLIGHTER:

They found me.
And I was sent back to the Plantations.
I remember what was going through
My head as I stood on those cobbles.
I knew exactly what I was going back to.
I remember
Standing there as if I had stopped time.

CONSTANCE:

I remember.

ALL:

West Indian Trade! East Indian Trade!
Baltic Trade!

CONSTANCE:

Money makes the world go round.

BLACK HARRIOT:

Money makes the man.

I remember once hearing BigCheese say
I would rather have my money buried with me
Than give it to the slave.

MARY:

And alas! I am weary, weary O.

CONSTANCE:

Money sets the world in motion.

MARY:

I came under the hammer for money.
I was money for old rope.

CONSTANCE:

My children were sold for money.

MARY:

The BigMan made millions out of me!

CONSTANCE:

Guinea, shilling, penny, florin.
Ingot, silver, copper, farthing.
Buck, fiver, tenner, pony.
Copper, sovereign, nickel, crown.
Quid, bob, bit, pound.

MARY:

Bigbelly made a mint out of me.

BLACK HARRIOT:

His ships came home.

MARY:

Bigbelly laughed all the way to the bank.

BLACK HARRIOT:

His ships came home.

MARY:

BigCheese raked it in.

CONSTANCE:

I cut the cane.

MARY:

Fatface made a fortune.

ALL:

And alas I am weary, weary O.

BLACK HARRIOT:

His ships came home.

SONG:

LAMPLIGHTER *(sings)*:

Look at the sugar ships cross the water.

ALL:

Hey nanny, ho nanny hey nanny no

BLACK HARRIOT:

Look at the big ship taking away my daughter

ALL:

Hey nanny, ho nanny, hey nanny no.

MARY:

There is not a brick in this city

CONSTANCE:

Huff puff. Blow your house down!

BLACK HARRIOT:

Bristol, London, Liverpool, Glasgow

MARY:
    There is not a brick in this city

LAMPLIGHTER:
    But what is cemented with the blood of a slave

CONSTANCE *(sings)*:
    Bristol belongs to me.

MACBEAN:
    I put them all in leg irons; and if that not
    Be enough, why then I handcuff them;
    If the handcuff be too little, I put
    A collar round their neck, with a chain
    Locked to a ring-bolt on the deck; if one chain
    Won't do, I put two, and if two won't do, three,
    You may trust me for that. These are not cruelties;
    They are matters of course. There is no carrying on
    The trade without them.

LAMPLIGHTER:
    May 22, 1731, the slave ship Neptune
    Of Port of Glasgow, dropped anchor in
    Carlisle Bay, Barbados.
    On board were 144 enslaved Africans
    Who had been shackled for nearly a year
    With leg irons.

MARY:
    And alas! I am weary, weary O

BLACK HARRIOT *(sings)*:
    I belong to Glasgow and Glasgow belongs to me!

LAMPLIGHTER:
    Some stories don't have a name to their voice.
    I built those houses, brick by brick.

BLACK HARRIOT:

My head is on the red brick Customs House in Liverpool in between the elephants.

LAMPLIGHTER:

The Tobacco Merchant's House, The Trades Hall,
The Gallery of Modern Art, Venturer's House:

BLACK HARRIOT:

London, Liverpool, Bristol, Manchester, Glasgow belongs to me!

CONSTANCE:

William Cowper,

BLACK HARRIOT:

the poet

MARY:

wrote

CONSTANCE:

I pity them greatly

BLACK HARRIOT:

meaning me

CONSTANCE:

I pity them greatly but I must be MUM
For how could we do without sugar and rum.

MACBEAN:

Instructions sent by the Bristol firm of Isaac Hobhouse. Let your knetting be fix'd breast high fore and aft and so keep 'em shackled and hand bolted. We hope this will find you with a fine parcel of Negroes ready to be put on board. Endeavour to purchase about 100 boys and girls from 10 to 14 years of age. Observe that the Boys and Girls you buy be very black and handsome.

CONSTANCE:

I landed in Barbados brought by the Royal Africa Company.
I was a child. One in six of us were children.

ANNIWAA:

I was a girl once. I wonder if I am still a girl. Maybe, not a girl
anymore. Maybe I have grown into a small woman without my
mother.

MARY:

I can hardly remember the girl I was or if I was ever a girl.

ANNIWAA:

I am the ghost of the child past. I am your past.

MARY:

I landed in Jamaica in the 1720s. I was a child. They named me
Mary MacDonald

MACBEAN:

In 1770 on the slave island of Jamaica
There were one hundred Black people
Called MacDonald;
A quarter of the island's people
Were Scottish.

BLACK HARRIOT:

My daughters have Scottish blood.
Scotland has my blood.

MACBEAN:

There was a network of Argyle Campbells at least 100 strong
in Jamaica. Concentrated in the west with place names such as
Campbell Town, Argyle and Glen Islay.

LAMPLIGHTER:

My story is the story of Great Britain
The United Kingdom, The British Empire

BLACK HARRIOT:

In 1756 in Liverpool, there was an auction at the Merchants' Coffee house for: 83 pairs of shackles, 11 slave collars, 22 pairs of handcuffs, 4 long chains, 34 rings and 2 travelling chains.

CONSTANCE:

1760. In London, an iron gag muzzle specially designed for use on Africans was offered for sale by ironmongers.

LAMPLIGHTER:

Chained two by two
Right leg and left leg
Right hand and left hand
Each African had less room
Than a man in a coffin.

ALL:

Boom! Boom! Boom!

Scene 14: Shipping News

MACBEAN (*slowly*):
> Buryed a man slave. Number 84.
> Buryed a boy slave no 47.
> Buryed a girl slave no 126.
> Finally. Into the seas. Moving steadily
> And filling. Cyclonic becoming Northwesterly.
> Severe Gale 9, Later.
> New High expected by same time tomorrow.

LAMPLIGHTER:
> By same time tomorrow.

MACBEAN (*despondent now*):
> The moon that night was cleaved in half,
> The night the ships landed in the Americas.
> The slaves were shined and sold.
> When the ships unloaded their slaves,
> The ship's shelves were reloaded with sugar,
> Tobacco, rum, heading for London, Liverpool,
> Glasgow. Rum weather.
> Moderate, not good. Fog thick as syrup.
> Visibility poor.
> Shannon. Rockall, West or Northwest,
> Backing Southwest 6 to 8.
> Occasionally very high in the West, sole.

LAMPLIGHTER:
> Becoming very Rough.
> Rough.
> Rough or very rough.
> Becoming very Rough.
> Rough, very Rough.
> Becoming very Rough.

MACBEAN:
> And that is the end of the shipping forecast.

Scene 15: Resistance

CONSTANCE:

> August 14th 1791. At a Voodoo service in Saint Dominique, a
> woman becomes possessed by Ogoun, the Voodoo warrior spirit.
> She sacrifices a black pig, and speaking in the voice of Ogoun,
> she names those who must lead the call for resistance.

(The women whisper to each other, plotting. Sound of burning, rackling, celebrating.)

MACBEAN:

> Made a timely discovery today that the slaves were forming a
> plot for insurrection. Punishment: Gelding or chopping of half
> of the foot with an axe.

CONSTANCE:

> The passing on, quick – quick, of an idea
> Is irrepressible.

LAMPLIGHTER:

> I can write it down! I will write it down and pass it on. This is
> a letter from me to my ancestors.

CONSTANCE:

> This is the story of the Lamplighter

LAMPLIGHTER:

> First, they wouldn't let me publish it.
> They tried to censor it.
> Eventually I managed it.

MACBEAN:

> Glasgow. 1792. 13,000 residents put their name to a petition
> drawn from a non-Conformist movement to abolish slavery.
> The movement to end slavery in the British Empire in the
> eighteenth century is likely the first human rights campaign in
> history.

BLACK HARRIOT:
  April 2nd 1792.

LAMPLIGHTER:
  Pitt to the House

MACBEAN:
  We may now consider this trade as having received its condem-
  nation;

CONSTANCE:
  Condemnation

MACBEAN:
  that its sentence is sealed;

MARY:
  Sealed!

MACBEAN:
  that this curse of mankind is seen by the House in its true light;

LAMPLIGHTER:
  true light

MACBEAN:
  and that the greatest stigma on our national character which ever
  yet existed, is about to be

BLACK HARRIOT:
  removed.

MACBEAN:
  And, Sir, I trust, we are now likely to be delivered from the
  greatest practical evil that ever has afflicted.

BLACK HARRIOT:
  the human race –

MACBEAN:

from the severest and most extensive calamity recorded in the history of the world!

LAMPLIGHTER:

Immediate, not gradual abolition!

BLACK HARRIOT:

Watch the fire spread!

CONSTANCE:

A rebellion could start in the north of the island
And move to the south in seconds –
Minutes, the fire of the idea sweeping faster
Than the bush

MUSIC:

(The sound of drums beating.)

BLACK HARRIOT:

We'd see the fire on the other plantations
And that was our sign!

MARY:

The Rebellion in Grenada

BLACK HARRIOT:

And the Rebellion in St Vincent

CONSTANCE:

Tacky's Rebellion, Jamaica

MARY:

Providence Rebellion

MACBEAN:

Am I not a man and a brother?

LAMPLIGHTER:

Am I not a woman and a sister?

MACBEAN:

Jan 1st 1804. Saint Dominique achieves the only completely successful slave rebellion in world history and becomes the Republic of Haiti.

In exchange for diplomatic recognition by Great Britain, Haiti must agree to pay France 150 million gold francs compensation for the loss of "property", including slaves.

LAMPLIGHTER:

Schools were closed. Education stopped. Freedom stopped.

MACBEAN:

It took Haiti one hundred years to pay the 'liberty debt'.

CONSTANCE:

One slave rebellion after another.

BLACK HARRIOT:

Bermuda.

MARY:

Boni Rebellion, Surinam.

CONSTANCE:

New River revolt, Belize.
Fedons rebellion, Grenada.

BLACK HARRIOT:

Getting – closer

MACBEAN:

On the 25th of March at Noon
the Bill to Abolish the British slave trade
is signed into law by George III.

BLACK HARRIOT:

What happened?

MARY:

What changed?

LAMPLIGHTER:

More slave ships sailed the shark filled sea.

CONSTANCE:

More beatings for you, for me.

FX:

(We hear cheering and celebrating in a distant country. Sound of drums.)

BLACK HARRIOT:

The Easter Rebellion, Barbados.
Second Maroon war, Jamaica.

MARY:

Cuffy Rebellion, Berbice.
Tula Rebellion, Curaçao.

CONSTANCE:

Coming soon.

BLACK HARRIOT:

The Demerara Rebellions.
Christmas revolt, Antigua.
St Kitts uprising.

MACBEAN:

Bee it enacted by the kings most excellent majestie that it shall not be lawfull for any negroe or other slave to goe or depart from his masters ground without a certificate from his master, mistris or overseer; and every negroe or slave soe offending shalbe sent to the next constable, who is hereby enjoyned and required to give the said negroe twenty lashes on his bare back well layd on.

CONSTANCE:

Pumpey's revolt Bahamas.
Uprising, Courland Bay, Tobago.
New year revolution, Dominica.

MARY:

One island after another.

BLACK HARRIOT:

Bring it on!

CONSTANCE:

Closer coming soon.

BLACK HARRIOT:

A tinder spark from one small island
Can easily land on another.
Bring out the conch shells and the horns!

MACBEAN:

Am I not a Man and a Brother?

LAMPLIGHTER:

Am I not a Woman and a Sister?

MARY:

Eventually, on my last legs
At the end of the day,
I was too tired to get away.
I kept the Lord beside me.
Amen.

BLACK HARRIOT:

I had my own spirit. I was never going to let them break me.

ANNIWAA:

All of a sudden, some men come and take us.

LAMPLIGHTER:

I was spirited away.

MARY:

In the name of the father, the Spirit and the Holy Ghost.

CONSTANCE:

My children were spirited away.

LAMPLIGHTER:

Am I not a Woman and a Sister?

MARY:

Am I not a Woman and a Sister!

BLACK HARRIOT:

Immediate, not gradual abolition!

MARY:

The Jamaican Christmas Revolt was organised by Sam Sharpe.

LAMPLIGHTER:

I'd rather die on yonder gallows than live in slavery.

MACBEAN:

The Revolt started in St James and spread through the whole island. It lasted eight days.

FX:

(Cane fields on fire.)

MACBEAN:

On Friday, July 26, 1833, the Bill for the Abolition of Slavery passes its second reading in the House of Commons after an agreement is reached to generously compensate the slave owners. 'Thank God,' says William Wilberforce, 'that I should live to witness a day in which England is willing to give twenty millions sterling for the Abolition of Slavery.'

SONG:

(Spiritual.)

ALL *(sing)*:

I went down in the valley one day
Good Lord, show me the way
Talking about that good old way,
Good Lord, show me the way.

LAMPLIGHTER:

On a sweltering night before the 1st of August 1838, the Baptist church in Falmouth, Jamaica, hung its walls with flowers. A coffin was inscribed: Colonial Slavery died July 31 1838.

The coffin was filled with British slavery – chains, collars, whips.

MUSIC

Scene 16: Freedom

LAMPLIGHTER:

This is the story of the Lamplighter:
One day, I finally managed to tell
My story. I wrote it down.
It was printed and reprinted
And told.
And retold again.

MARY:

At the end of the long day
I found a free man
Who loved me, even though
I was scarred all over.
He'd kiss me gently,
And hold my rough hands
To his face.
His voice was rich, melodious.
He tried to buy my freedom
FatMan wouldn't let me go.

BLACK HARRIOT:

My children
Were his children.
I could always see his eyes in their eyes.
I don't know where they've gone.
What's become of them.
(With bravado.)
They haven't had anything
I didn't have.
I never knew *my* mother.
And I managed. Life's tough!

SONG:

(Spiritual repeated.)

ALL *(sings)*:
I went down in the valley one day
Good Lord, show me the way
Talking about that good old way,
Good Lord, show me the way.

CONSTANCE:
My children are scattered,
Maybe dead, maybe alive.
I wonder if I will ever see my wise boy,
My bean girl, if they'll ever
Try and come and find me.

LAMPLIGHTER:
And one day the years caught up with me
I turned round, and there they were,
All the years,

ANNIWAA:
There I was

LAMPLIGHTER:
The years, facing me. Her hair plaited with thread. She has
climbed down from the tree. She is wearing her mother's yellow
head-tie. Her arms on her hips

BLACK HARRIOT:
Eyes steady

MARY:
Mouth open

CONSTANCE:
Words ready

ANNIWAA:
To be spoken

BLACK HARRIOT:
    This is not the end

LAMPLIGHTER:
    Only when I turned and faced her,
    Standing there like that,
    Could I begin to tell this story.

ANNIWAA:
    I am a girl. I am in the dark. I don't know how long I've been
    kept in the dark. High above me, there is a tiny crack of light.
    Last time I counted, I was eleven, nearly twelve.

CONSTANCE:
    Eventually I got my freedom.
    I had to work to buy my shack,
    Had to pay them back for
    My own work!
    I became Aunty to all the children.

    All children are my grandchildren.
    Sometimes I tell them the stories.
    Sometimes, I sit quiet.
    I'm just hearing where the breeze is coming from.

MARY:
    You know the funny thing?
    Big Man is dead. Houselady dead.
    The driver is dead. The overseer man passed
    Away last autumn. And me Mary
    Who hardly ate a thing
    And was beaten till
    An inch of my life.
    I survived! Trust in Jesus!
    I survived them all.

LAMPLIGHTER:
    Nobody told my story.

ANNIWAA:

I don't know how long I'll be kept in the dark.

ALL:

HushShhhhhhhhhhhhhhhhhhhhhhhh.

MACBEAN:

She never said a word.

LAMPLIGHTER:

This is my story.

ANNIWAA:

I am a girl.

CONSTANCE:

One day I would like to tell my grandchildren.
If I could find them; I would tell them.

BLACK HARRIOT:

This sure as hell is my story!

MARY:

This happened to me, the Lord knows it's the truth.

ANNIWAA:

Once upon a time, I lived in a house with a cone-shaped roof, in a big compound. My mother grew okra and pumpkin in her yard. My father shaped woods and metals.

USEFUL SOURCES & FURTHER READING

Quobna Ottobah Cugoano: *Thoughts and Sentiments on the Evil of Slavery* (Penguin Classics)

Olaudah Equiano: *The Interesting Narrative of the Life of Olaudah Equiano: Written by Himself* (Wilder Publications)

The Narrative of Sojourner Truth Dictated by Sojourner Truth (Penguin Classics)

The History of Mary Prince: A West Indian Slave related by Herself (Wilder Publications)

Afua Cooper: *The Hanging of Angelique: the untold story of Canadian Slavery* (University of Georgia Press)

Hugh Thomas: *The Slave Trade: The History of the Atlantic Slave Trade* (Simon & Schuster)

Adam Hochschild: *Bury the Chains* (Houghton Mifflin)

C.L.R. James: *The Black Jacobins: Toussaint L'Ouverture and the San Domingo Revolution* (Vintage)

Eric Williams: *Capitalism and Slavery* (Cambridge University Press)

James Walvin: *Britain's Slave Empire* (Wiley-Blackwell)

James Walvin: *Black Ivory: History of British Slavery* (Fontana)

Robin Blackburn: *The Overthrow of Colonial Slavery 1776-1848* (Verso)

Hilary Beckles: *Natural Rebels: A Social History of Enslaved Black Women in Barbados* (Rutgers University Press)

Lucille Mathurin Mair, Hilary Beckles & Verene A. Shepherd: *Historical Study of Women in Jamaica, 1655-1844* (University of West Indies Press)

Catherine Hall: *White, Male, and Middle Class: Explorations in Feminism and History* (Polity Press)

Joseph Opala: *The Gullah: Rice, slavery and the Sierra Leone-American connection* (USIS)

Nigel Pocock: *Liverpool Boom, People and Places Connected with Slavery in Liverpool and Lancaster* (Soma Books Ltd)

S.D. Smith: *Slavery, Family, and Gentry Capitalism in the British Atlantic* (Cambridge University Press)

Madge Dresser: *Slavery Obscured: The Social History of the Slave Trade in an English Provincial Port* (Continuum International Publishing Group)

S.I. Martin: *Britain's Slave Trade* (Channel 4 Books)

Guy Grannum: *Tracing Your West Indian Ancestors* (Public Record Office Publications)

Pam Fraser Solomon: *Enslavement a Timeline*

Simon Schama: *Rough Crossings: Britain, the Slaves and the American Revolution* (Eco)

Trade and Empire: Remembering Slavery (Whitworth Art Gallery, Manchester), curators Su Andi, Kevin R.U. Dalton-Johnson, Emma Poulter and Dr Alan Rice

WEBSITES

BBC History: http://www.bbc.co.uk/history/british/abolition/

Museum in Dockland: London, Sugar & Slavery: http://www.museumindocklands.org.uk

Bryan Mawer, Sugar Refiners & Sugarbakers: http://www.mawer.clara.net/intro.html

Lifeline: The March of the Abolitionist: http://www.lifelineexpedition.co.uk/mota/index.htm

Anti-Slavery International: Rendezvous of Victory: http://www.antislavery.org/

Mia Morris: http://www.black-history-month.co.uk/

International Slavery Museum, Liverpool: http://www.liverpoolmuseums.org.uk/ism/

English Heritage: Slavery and Justice Exhibition at Kenwood House: http://www.english-heritage.org.uk/server/show/ConWebDoc.13404

UNESCO: Breaking the Silence – The ASPnet Transatlantic Slave Trade Project: http://portal.unesco.org/education/